15 ESSENTIAL FORMULAS TO ACHIEVE FINANCIAL SECURITY: Tested Techniques for Generating, Preserving, and Savoring Enduring Fortune

Lynn D. Battle

Copyright ©

All rights reserved. No part of this publication may be reproduced, distributed, or transmitted in any form or by any means, including photocopying, recording, or other electronic or mechanical methods, without the prior written permission of the publisher, except in the case of brief quotations embodied in critical reviews and certain other noncommercial uses permitted by copyright law.

Copyright © Lynn D. Battle, 2024.

Table of contents
Introduction
Chapter 1
Financial Security
Chapter 2
The Income Formula
Chapter 3
The Savings Formula
Chapter 4
The Investment Formula
Chapter 5
The Budgeting Formula
Chapter 6
The Debt Management Formula
Chapter 7
The Insurance Formula
Chapter 8
The Tax Optimization Formula
Chapter 9
The Retirement Planning Formula
Chapter 10
The Formula for Building Wealth
Chapter 11
The Financial Education Formula
Chapter 12
The Asset Protection Formula
Chapter 13

The Financial Discipline Formula
Chapter 14
The Formula for Preserving Wealth
Chapter 15
The Financial Freedom Formula
Chapter 16
The Legacy Planning Formula
CONCLUSION

Introduction

The pursuit of financial independence and security is more important than ever in a society where such things sometimes seem unattainable. Many individuals find it difficult to make sense of the complicated world of personal finance and struggle with issues related to investing, saving budgeting, and future planning. While achieving financial stability may seem impossible, it is possible if you have the appropriate information and techniques.

The in-depth manual "15 Essential Formulas to Achieve Financial Security" can help you attain long-term financial independence and stability. The goal of this book is to make the process easier by reducing the key elements of financial stability to 15 practical formulae. Each formula helps you create, protect, and enjoy your money by providing a methodical approach based on proven financial concepts.

What Benefits You?

You will have a comprehensive grasp of the procedures required to attain financial stability by the conclusion of this book. You'll discover how to make well-informed choices that support your objectives, manage your money more skillfully, and experience less financial stress. More significantly, with a strong strategy in place, you'll feel empowered to take charge of your financial destiny.

Recall that achieving financial stability does not need sudden achievement or easy remedies. It all comes down to using the appropriate tactics consistently over time. This book's formulae are designed to be both flexible and sustainable, so you can keep your financial situation stable no matter what changes life throws at you.

Are you prepared to start along the path to financial stability now? Now let's explore the formulae that will help you along the way.

Chapter 1

Financial Security

"Being able to pay for your bills without experiencing worry is the essence of financial stability."

What is Financial Security?
Financial security may be defined practically as feeling in control of your finances generally, saving enough money for emergencies, managing debt responsibly, and spending less than you make.

Why Does Having Financial Security Matter?
A satisfying life is strongly based on financial stability, which has many advantages that go beyond just being monetary. Here are three strong arguments for why it's so crucial:

- **Tranquility of mind:** The comfort that comes with having financial stability helps to reduce the worry and anxiety that come with not having enough money. It offers a safety net for unforeseen costs and crises.

- **Independence and Freedom:** Financially secure people can make decisions that are consistent with their ideals and objectives. It gives individuals the freedom to follow their interests, take measured chances, and live more independently.

- **Forward-Looking Scheduling:** A stable financial base enables people to make plans. Achieving long-term objectives, like as having a family, purchasing a house, or retiring comfortably, is made possible by financial stability.

In conclusion, financial security is essentially the stability and assurance that come from knowing you have enough money to meet your present and future demands. This entails having a reliable source of income, a planned spending plan, investments, savings, and insurance to guard against unexpected events. However, each technique for achieving financial stability will be presented in the next chapters.

Chapter 2

The Income Formula

"The foundation of all your financial development is your revenue. With careful care, it will provide a crop of freedom and security."

Income: What Is It?
What you are paid for commodities, labor, or services is called income. Still, it is the cornerstone of financial stability. It is practically difficult to invest, save, or make plans without a consistent and substantial source of income. However, money isn't just about how much you earn; it's also about how you can grow, safeguard, and produce it.

Recognizing the Significance of Income
The source of every other financial activity is income. It powers your investments, sustains your savings, pays off your obligations, and finances your lifestyle. While many people concentrate on cutting costs to manage their money, raising your income may have a more substantial effect. Greater income translates into increased chances for investing, saving, and achieving financial independence.

The Income Formula consists of three main parts.
1. **Revenue from Activities**
   The most prevalent kind of income is active income, which usually originates from a job or self-employment. It is the money you get in return for the benefits you provide to society or the values you uphold. It may come from your earnings, salary, or contract job.

   Here are some strategies to increase your current income:
   - **Career Advancement:** To grow in your career, invest in your education and skill set. Ask for increases, pursue promotions, and always work to increase your worth as a professional.

   - **Adjacent Businesses:** Look into other sources of income than your main employment. This may include starting a small company, consulting, or freelancing.

   - **Networking:** Create a strong professional network that may open doors to new employment prospects, profitable side gigs, or income-boosting collaborations.

2. **Income from Passive Sources**

   These are profits, like rental income, dividends, or royalties, that come in with little to no continuous work. Passive income earns money without requiring you to put in as much continuing labor as active income does.

   Long-term financial stability depends on creating passive income streams, which enable you to make money even while you're not working. Here are a few strategies for generating side income:
   - **Investments:** Make interest- or dividend-paying stock, bond, or mutual fund investments. These assets may increase in value over time and provide a consistent flow of income.

   - **Real Estate:** Invest in rental properties that bring in money each month. A strong strategy for accumulating money and ensuring a steady income is via real estate.

   - **Digital Products:** Produce and market digital goods that need little work to maintain over time, such as software, e-books, and courses.

- **Royalties:** Get paid for creative activity like authoring a book, making music, or producing intellectual property that may be licensed for a profit.

3. **The act of diversification**

   This entails diversifying sources of income to lower risk and improve financial stability.

   Dependence on one source of income alone may be dangerous. Your financial stability may be swiftly jeopardized by industry demand shifts, job losses, or economic downturns. It is important to diversify your sources of income to reduce these dangers.

   Here's how to successfully diversify:
   - **Several Revenue Streams:** Make an effort to create several revenue streams. You may, for instance, earn money from investments, a rental property, and full-time work. This way, you have alternative sources of income to fall back on in case one is interrupted.

   - **Industry Diversification:** Take into account prospects for revenue across many sectors. If technology is your main line of work, you may go into real estate or healthcare investments. This lessens your susceptibility to downturns unique to your sector.

- **Geographic Diversification:** If at all feasible, distribute your sources of income across other nations or areas. This might shield your income from regional economic problems.

Methods for Raising Revenue

Leveraging your abilities, taking advantage of opportunities, and making calculated choices to increase your financial resources are the key components of increasing your income. It entails figuring out how to optimize your earning potential, whether it is by developing numerous revenue sources, investing sensibly, or progressing in your job. The secret is to always provide value and look for opportunities that fit your objectives and dreams.

The precise tactics listed below may help you raise your income:

- **Reskilling and Upskilling:** Maintain your competitiveness in the labor market by always improving your abilities. Think about enrolling in classes, obtaining certificates, or picking up new, in-demand technology.

- **Bargaining:** Do not be afraid to bargain for your pay or other expenses. Examine industry norms and be ready to defend your value to potential employers or clients.

- **Entrepreneurship:** Think about launching your own company if you have a talent or passion that can be made profitable. Though there are dangers involved, being an entrepreneur may be a great way to boost your income.

- **Investment in Income-Generating Assets:** Set aside a percentage of your earnings to put toward stocks, bonds, real estate, or company ventures as investments that will increase your income.

Safeguarding Your Income

It's important to safeguard your income even as you strive to increase and diversify it. The following are some methods to protect your income:

- **Emergency Fund:** Establish and keep an emergency fund large enough to pay for costs for three to six months. This will prevent you from having to liquidate your assets to handle financial shocks like job loss or unforeseen bills. Make sure you have sufficient insurance coverage, such as life, health, and disability insurance. These may safeguard your income in the case of a disease, accident, or demise.

- **Legal Protections:** To secure your income from litigation and creditors, think about creating an LLC or establishing trusts if you own a company or substantial assets.

Generally speaking, money is the cornerstone of your financial stability, but it goes beyond just receiving a salary. Through comprehension and implementation of the Income Formula, which involves optimizing active income generation, cultivating passive income, and broadening your sources of revenue, you may establish a sturdy financial base that sustains your objectives and endures economic oscillations.

Chapter 3

The Savings Formula

"Like water in a bucket with a steady leak, the value of savings without investment gradually decreases."

One essential component of financial stability is saving money. While having a source of money is vital, what you do with it is just as significant. Saving money not only helps you plan for future objectives and crises, but it also establishes the foundation for investing, which is essential to accumulating wealth.

The Mentality of Preservation

Understanding the psychology of saving is crucial before delving into its mechanics. It takes discipline, postponing pleasure, and having a clear idea of your financial objectives to save money. Saving often requires forgoing new pleasures in favor of future gains, which is why many individuals find it difficult to save. You may, however, develop a habit of saving that seems both satisfying and doable by changing your perspective and concentrating on the long-term gains.

The Savings Formula's Elements

Three fundamental elements form the foundation of the Savings Formula:
1. **Clearly Defined Savings Objectives**
   The absence of specific objectives is one of the main barriers to saving. Savings without a clear goal might seem pointless and uninspiring. To start overcoming this, make sure your savings objectives are specific, quantifiable, and time-bound. Here's how to do it:
   - **Short-Term Objectives:** These may include putting money aside for presents for the holidays, a new device, or a trip. Short-term objectives demand a more concentrated approach to saving and usually last shorter than a year.

   - **Medium-Term Objectives:** These may include saving money for a down payment on a home, a vehicle, or more schooling. Typically, medium-term objectives last one to five years.

   - **Long-Term Objectives:** Major life events like retirement or your child's schooling are often linked to long-term objectives. These long-term, multi-decade objectives need constant, disciplined saving.

Use the SMART criteria (Specific, Measurable, Achievable, Relevant, and Time-bound) to develop savings objectives that are realistic. A SMART goal would be, for instance, "save $500 per month for retirement to reach $300,000 in 20 years," as opposed to a general objective like "save for retirement."

2. **Establishing an Emergency Reserve**

    One of the most important elements of financial stability is an emergency fund. It serves as a safety net against unforeseen expenses like job loss, necessary home repairs, or medical crises. It also offers a financial peace of mind. This is how you create a substantial emergency fund:

    I. **Establish a Specific Objective**

    Ascertain the amount that you must save first. Generally speaking, you should aim to save three to six months' worth of living expenditures. Essentials like rent or a mortgage, utilities, food, transportation, and insurance should be covered by this sum. You may want to aim toward the upper end of this range if you have dependents or a changeable income.

II. **Establish a Different Account**
Store your emergency money in a different, conveniently located account. Because it provides higher interest rates than a standard savings account and yet permits easy access to your money when required, a high-yield savings account is an excellent choice. To avoid the temptation to spend this money on non-emergencies, do not store it in your bank account.

III. **Begin Little and Continue Regularly**
Start by putting away a little sum regularly, even if it's just $20 or $50 a week. Maintaining consistency is essential. Savings automation may help streamline this procedure. To make sure you're always contributing, set up automatic transfers from your checking account to your emergency fund every payday.

IV. **Modify Your Spending Plan**
Find places where you can make savings in your budget so that you can add to your emergency fund more quickly. This might

include cutting down on discretionary spending on entertainment, eating out, and shopping. Put the savings you made in these areas straight into your emergency savings.

V. **Set Fund Priorities**
Consider the amount in your emergency fund as a fixed expenditure. Verify that you have contributed to your money for the month before making any payments for non-essential things. If you happen to have a windfall, such as a bonus or tax return, think about contributing a sizeable amount to your emergency fund.

VI. **Evaluate and Modify**
Your demands for an emergency fund may vary as your circumstances change throughout life. Check your money regularly to make sure it still fits your needs and your current way of life. Make necessary adjustments to your savings target if your costs rise.

VII. **Make Good Use of It**
Use your emergency money only in cases of genuine need. This covers

unanticipated, urgent, and required circumstances, such as expensive auto repair or unforeseen medical expenses. After utilizing your savings to keep your safety net in place, replenish it as soon as you can.

VIII. **Honor significant anniversaries**
Achieving savings goals for your emergency fund is a noteworthy accomplishment. Recognize your advancement to maintain motivation. Every step you take toward achieving financial serenity, whether it's saving your first $500 or financing your whole goal, counts.

You may develop a cushion that can help you handle financial setbacks without jeopardizing your long-term objectives by meticulously creating and managing an emergency fund. It's an essential component of any sound financial strategy, providing you with the assurance that you're ready for everything that life may throw at you.

3. Setting Up Auto-Deposits

Automating the procedure is among the best strategies to regularly save money. Automation guarantees that saving becomes a regular part of your daily routine and eliminates the temptation to spend money that should be saved.

How to Set Up Auto-Savings

- **Create Automatic Transfers:** You may create automatic transfers from your checking and savings accounts to most banks and other organizations. Choose how much you want to save and set up a transfer to happen every payday or once a month, depending on how your money comes in.

- **Use Direct Deposit Splits:** You may transfer a part of your paycheck into your savings account immediately from your paycheck, if your company permits it. In this manner, your savings and spending money are automatically segregated.

- **Automate Retirement funds:** Take into consideration setting up your 401(k) or IRA to automatically deduct funds. Payroll deductions for retirement accounts are provided by many workplaces, which makes it simple to save regularly for the future.

- **Make Use of Savings Applications:** Several applications may assist in automating the savings process. Certain applications allow you to round up your purchases to the closest dollar and deposit the difference into your savings. Others let you program automatic transfers according to your spending patterns.

Techniques for Saving Money Effectively

Apart from establishing objectives, accumulating an emergency fund, and automating your savings, other tactics might enhance your ability to save efficiently:

a. **Pay Yourself First:** Just like rent or utilities, see your savings as a cost that must be avoided. Setting savings above other costs helps you stay on course to meet your financial objectives.

b. **Reducing Unnecessary Expenses:** Examine your monthly spending to find places where you might make savings. Use these funds to further your financial objectives.

c. **Increase Savings with Raises:** Rather than increasing your expenditures, think about setting aside some of your increase or bonus. In this manner, your savings and income increase together.

d. **Review and Modify Your Savings Strategy:** Review your financial objectives and progress regularly. As circumstances in life change, so should your savings strategy. Being adaptable is essential, whether it's raising your savings rate after debt repayment or changing your objectives after a significant life event.

Interest's Function in Savings

Especially in the long run, interest may have a big impact on how rapidly your funds increase. How to maximize it is as follows:

a. **High-Yield Savings Accounts:** Choose a savings account with a competitive interest rate. Even while savings accounts sometimes provide smaller returns than investments, any interest is beneficial over time, particularly when compounded.

b. **Certificates of Deposit (CDs):** You may want to put away any funds you don't need to access right away in a CD. CDs lock up your money for a certain amount of time in return for greater interest rates than traditional savings accounts.

c. **Compound Interest:** The ability to generate interest on interest is what gives compound interest its strength. The benefits of compounding increase with the age of your savings. For instance, after ten years, $10,000 in savings multiplied by a 2% annual interest rate and compounded annually would equal around $12,190.

Overcoming Typical Savings Obstacles

Saving money is important, but it's not always simple. The following are some typical obstacles individuals run into while attempting to conserve money, along with solutions:

a. **Lack of Motivation:** Divide the goal into smaller, more manageable milestones if you find it difficult to save because it appears too far off. Celebrate your accomplishments to stay inspired.

b. **Impulse Spending:** You shouldn't let impulsive purchases throw off your savings strategy. Make a 24-hour rule where you don't buy anything non-essential for a day to counteract this. This break typically prevents impulsive purchases.

c. **Inconsistent Income:** Saving money might be difficult if your income is erratic, as it can be from freelancing or another source. Here, your goal should be to save a portion of your income as opposed to a certain sum. Save more during months of strong income to offset months of low income.

d. **Debt Prioritization:** It might be difficult to strike a balance between saving and paying off debt. Give high-interest debt a priority, but don't completely ignore your savings. Regular savings contributions, even in small amounts, can help you stay on target.

Furthermore, the Savings Formula focuses on building a safety net for finances, establishing specific objectives, and forming long-term financial security-promoting behaviors in addition to just laying away money. You may integrate saving into your financial life by automating your savings, creating an emergency fund, and establishing clear objectives.

Chapter 4

The Investment Formula

"Real investment is in the idea of what you can create, not simply in cash. Allow the decisions you make now to shape tomorrow's riches and knowledge."

The secret to accumulating money and securing your financial future is investing. While investing enables your money to grow and work for you over time, saving is necessary for emergencies and short-term objectives. When paired with wise investment choices, the potential of compounding returns may greatly improve your financial situation. Moreover, investing may be used to reach short- or long-term financial objectives, maintain buying power, and increase wealth.

The Value of Financial Investing

Investing is an essential part of anyone's financial strategy, not simply those who are affluent or financially astute. Over time, inflation reduces the buying power of money, so just putting money in a low-interest savings account would not be sufficient to keep up with growing expenses. Whether your financial objectives are to support your education, purchase a house, or ensure a comfortable retirement, investing may help you reach your financial goals and increase your wealth.

The Elements of the Formula for Investing

Three fundamental elements form the foundation of the Investment Formula:

1. **Being Aware of Various Investment Types**

    Because there are so many alternatives to choose from, investing may seem daunting. You may, however, make more educated choices if you are aware of the fundamental kinds of investments and how they operate. The most popular investment categories are as follows:

    - **Stocks:** Purchasing stocks entitles you to ownership shares in a business. While stocks may provide large gains, there is a greater risk associated with them. The success of the business and general market circumstances may have an impact on the value of your investment.

    - **Bonds:** Issued by governments or businesses, bonds are debt instruments. Purchasing a bond is equivalent to lending money to the issuer in return for regular interest payments and the repayment of the bond's face value when it matures. Although they provide smaller returns than stocks, bonds are often seen to be less risky.

- **Mutual Funds:** To buy a diverse portfolio of stocks, bonds, and other assets, mutual funds combine the money of many individuals. Although they incur management fees, mutual funds, which are overseen by qualified portfolio managers, provide a simple means of diversifying your assets.

- **Exchange-Traded Funds (ETFs):** ETFs trade on stock exchanges like individual equities, yet they resemble mutual funds. Compared to mutual funds, they usually have cheaper costs and provide diversity.

- **Real estate:** Investing in real estate is buying property to resell or selling it for a profit down the road. While it takes a lot of money and effort, real estate can be a very effective vehicle for accumulating wealth.

- **Commodities:** Physical things like gold, oil, and agricultural products are examples of commodities. Commodity prices might fluctuate, but investing in them can provide diversity and serve as a hedge against inflation.

- **Cryptocurrencies:** Although they carry a large degree of risk and volatility, virtual currencies like Bitcoin and Ethereum have the potential to provide large rewards. Since cryptocurrency investment is still in its infancy, care should be used.

- **Alternative Investments:** These include securities such as hedge funds, private equity, and collectibles (such as artwork and antiques). Although they are sometimes more complicated and less liquid than conventional investments, alternative investments may provide diversity.

2. **Diversification and Risk Management**
Recognizing the link between risk and return is a fundamental aspect of investing. increased potential returns are usually accompanied by increased risks. Thus, a good investing strategy must include excellent risk management.

- **Diversification:** This refers to distributing your assets across many asset classes, including bonds, equities, and real estate, as well as throughout various sectors and geographical areas within those classes. The idea is to lessen the effect that any one investment has on your portfolio as a whole. The performance of your portfolio may be stabilized, for instance, if you own a diverse mix of assets, since gains in one sector may offset declines in another.

- **Asset Allocation:** This approach divides your assets across several asset classes according to your personal risk tolerance, time horizon for making investments, and financial goals. A younger investor with a longer time horizon may devote a larger portion of their portfolio to equities due to their greater potential for growth at the expense of more volatility. In contrast, to protect money and provide a consistent income stream, an older investor who is getting close to retirement may place a higher priority on bonds and other income-producing assets.

- **Rebalancing:** Your asset allocation may deviate from its intended goal when the value of your assets changes over time. Rebalancing is the practice of regularly modifying your portfolio to keep the asset mix that you have chosen. For instance, you may decide to sell some stocks and put money into bonds to bring your portfolio back into balance if equities do better than expected and take up a larger percentage of it.

- **Risk Tolerance:** Developing an effective investing plan requires an understanding of your risk tolerance, or the amount of risk you are willing and able to accept. Your choice of assets and asset allocation will be determined by your level of risk tolerance. A conservative portfolio with a greater emphasis on bonds and lower-risk assets may be more appealing to you if you are risk-averse. You may choose a more aggressive strategy with a higher allocation to stocks if you are comfortable taking on risk.

3. **Formulating an Extended-Term Investment Plan**

To secure your financial future and achieve significant financial development, you must develop a long-term investing plan. This strategy calls for thorough preparation and a long-term dedication to sticking to your investing plan. Here's how to create a successful long-term investing plan:

- **Set Clear Goals:** To begin, decide what your financial objectives are. These might include accumulating money, purchasing a property, paying for a child's education, and saving for retirement. Your investing plan will be shaped and motivated by well-defined objectives. To help you plan, set SMART (specific, measurable, realistic, relevant, and time-bound) objectives.

- **Determine Your Risk Tolerance:** Be aware of how much you are willing and able to withstand changes in the market. Your investing time horizon, financial status, and degree of comfort with market volatility all have an impact on your risk tolerance. Understanding your risk tolerance can help you make investing decisions that are consistent with your ability to absorb possible losses.

- **Establish Your Time Horizon:** Your approach will be impacted by your investing time horizon, or the amount of time you want to keep assets before requiring the money. Since you have more time to recover from market downturns, longer time horizons usually allow for more aggressive investing. To safeguard your cash, shorter time horizons can need a more cautious strategy.

- **Select an Asset Allocation:** Create a diversified portfolio that takes your time horizon and risk tolerance into account. Investing in a variety of asset types, including cash, stocks, bonds, and real estate, is known as asset allocation. Within these asset types, diversification may help lower risk even further. Younger investors, for instance, could allocate more to stocks because of their greater growth potential, but those who are nearing retirement might choose bonds because of their stability and income.

- **Build a Diversified Portfolio:** To distribute risk across many assets, create a diversified portfolio. If one asset class underperforms, diversification can shield your portfolio from suffering substantial losses. Think about diversifying by sector, industry, and geographic area in addition to asset type.

- **Establish a Regular Investment Plan:** Decide on a regular investment plan that involves investing a certain amount at regular periods. An approach like this is called dollar-cost averaging. This method may help build wealth gradually over time and lessen the effects of market volatility. Set up an automated investing strategy to stay consistent and steer clear of irrational decisions.

- **Keep an eye on and Adjust Your Portfolio:** Make sure your portfolio is still in line with your investing objectives and risk tolerance by reviewing it regularly. Your asset allocation may deviate from your goal due to market movements. Rebalancing is bringing your portfolio back to its initial allocation to preserve the risk and return that you had planned.

- **Remain Educated and Flexible:** Stay up to date on market developments, financial situations, and adjustments to your situation. Even if your long-term strategy should stay the same, be ready to modify it in reaction to important life events or big changes in the financial environment.

- **Seek Professional Advice:** If you're unclear about your approach or want direction on difficult investing choices, think to consider speaking with a financial adviser. An adviser may assist in customizing your investment strategy to meet your specific goals and circumstances by offering professional advice and insights.

- **Remain Patient and Disciplined:** Patience and discipline are essential for long-term investment. Refrain from hastily responding to transient market swings and maintain your attention on your long-term objectives. With patience and faithfulness to your plan, you may see significant improvement over time.

You may achieve your financial objectives and accumulate money by creating and following a long-term investment plan. The secret is to negotiate shifting market conditions and situations with patience, knowledge, and smart modifications as required.

Typical Investment Techniques
Here are a few well-liked investing techniques to think about:

a. Investing in index funds or exchange-traded funds (ETFs) that follow a market index, such as the S&P 500, is known as **Index investing**. A passive approach with minimal costs, diversity, and wide market exposure is index investing.

b. **Dividend Investing:** This approach is centered on making dividend-paying company investments. A consistent income stream and the possibility of capital growth are offered by this approach.

c. **Worth Investing:** Purchasing cheap stocks that are thought to be selling below their true worth is known as value investing. The theory is that these equities will ultimately increase in value and provide a profit.

d. **Growth Investing:** This strategy focuses on businesses that are anticipated to expand at a higher pace than the market as a whole. Even though these businesses don't pay dividends, they reinvest profits to support expansion.

e. **Real estate investment:** This kind of investing is purchasing real estate to capitalize on growth or rental revenue. Real estate may be classified as either residential, commercial, or industrial.

f. **Socially Responsible Investing (SRI):** This entails selecting assets according to social, ethical, and environmental standards. SRI investors aim to provide financial rewards in addition to beneficial effects.

You may create a portfolio that supports your financial objectives and safeguards your future by learning about the many investment kinds, reducing risk via diversification, and formulating a long-term investing plan.

Chapter 5

The Budgeting Formula

"The art of budgeting consists in establishing and attaining financial objectives."

The cornerstone of financial stability is **Budgeting**. It's the tool that assists you in controlling your spending, managing your income, and choosing how you want to spend your money. Even the strongest income, savings, and investment plans may go south without a budget.

To ensure that you live within your means and optimize your capacity to save and invest, the Budgeting Formula is intended to assist you in developing a plan that matches your spending with your financial objectives.

The Value of Setting Up a Budget

A budget is a guide for your financial life, not merely a list of statistics. It offers you financial management, assisting with debt avoidance, future savings, and stress reduction. By prioritizing your expenses, budgeting helps you make sure that your money is spent on the things that are most important to you. Making a budget is crucial to reaching your financial objectives, whether they are saving for the future, paying off debt, or creating an emergency fund.

The Elements of the Formula for Budgeting

The four main parts of the budgeting formula are as follows:

1. **Monitoring Earnings and Outlays**

    Keeping track of your income and spending is the first step towards understanding your current financial condition and developing a budget. This entails determining all revenue streams and recording all outlays, regardless of size, including:

    - **Money Tracking:** To begin, make a list of all the sources of your money, such as investments, freelancing, rental income, and your pay. Don't forget to account for sporadic as well as consistent revenue. If your income fluctuates, use the lowest anticipated amount as a cautious estimate or an average based on previous months.

    - **Expense Tracking:** After that, to get a precise image of your spending patterns, keep a close eye on your outlays for a minimum of one month. This covers both variable and fixed costs (such as food, entertainment, and eating out) as well as fixed expenditures (such as rent, mortgage, and insurance). To keep track of all of your expenses, use a journal, spreadsheet, or budgeting tool. The objective is to track every dollar you spend so you can see exactly how much you're spending.

- **Finding Patterns:** After keeping tabs on your earnings and outlays, examine the information to find trends in your spending. Do you often overpay in any areas? Could you cut any discretionary spending? You may establish budget restrictions with the assistance of this study.

2. **Organizing Spending**
Having a good grasp of your income and spending patterns can help you classify your costs. You may better arrange your spending by grouping purchases according to your financial priorities by categorizing them.

    - **Needs versus desires:** Begin by classifying your spending into two categories: needs (non-essential costs like eating out, entertainment, and hobbies) and desires (necessary costs like housing, utilities, food, and transportation). Making changes as needed and prioritizing your expenditures depend heavily on this difference.

- **Fixed vs. Variable costs:** Fixed costs, like rent or vehicle payment, are ones that don't change from month to month. Variable expenses include food, utilities, and entertainment. Organizing spending in this manner makes it easier to spot places where you may make cost reductions.

- **Savings and Investments:** Remember to include these crucial budget areas in your plan. To guarantee that you constantly contribute to your financial objectives, see them as non-negotiable costs, similar to your rent or mortgage.

- **Debt Repayment:** Sort your payments according to the kind of outstanding debt you have, such as mortgages, credit card bills, and school loans. Making debt repayment a priority is crucial, particularly for high-interest debt, since it will free up more cash for future investments and savings.

3. **Establishing Budgetary Boundaries**
Setting budget boundaries for each area is the next step after classifying your costs. Budget limitations are constraints on your spending that help you arrange money according to your goals and make sure you don't spend more than you make.

- **The 50/30/20 Rule:** This well-liked budgeting technique allots 50% of your income to necessities, 30% to desires, and 20% to debt reduction and savings. This guideline offers a structure that is adaptable for handling your money while making sure you invest and save for the future.

- **Zero-Based Budgeting:** This method entails assigning a purpose to each dollar of your income to reduce your budget to zero by the end of the month. This approach guarantees that no money is left unallocated and pushes you to be deliberate with your spending.

- **Prioritizing Necessary Expenses:** Begin by establishing spending limits for your necessities, which include housing, utilities, and food. Before assigning money for discretionary expenditure, be sure these expenses are met.

- **Making Adjustments for Flexibility:** You should have adequate room in your budget for unforeseen costs or changes in your income. By modestly underestimating your income or overestimating your costs, you may add wiggle room to your budget.

4. **Consistently Examining and Modifying Your Budget**

   A budget should change as your financial circumstances do; it is not a static document. Maintaining a budget that is in line with your objectives and takes into account modifications to your income, spending, or priorities requires regular evaluation and adjustment.

   - **Monthly Check-Ins:** Evaluate how successfully you followed your spending limitations by looking over your budget at the end of each month. In what areas did you overspend? Did you have any unforeseen costs that you needed to pay for? Make changes based on this information for the next month.

- **Yearly assessment:** Perform a thorough yearly assessment of your budget in addition to monthly check-ins. Any major life events, like getting married, having a kid, or starting a new work, should be taken into account in this assessment, along with how they will affect your financial objectives.

- **Changing Your objectives:** Your objectives should adapt to your changing financial condition. Your budget should be adjusted to include additional money for savings, investments, or other financial objectives if you obtain a raise or pay off debt.

- **Remaining Flexible:** Since life is unpredictable, your spending plan should be adaptable. Your budget should be flexible enough to handle unforeseen expenses like auto repairs, medical bills, and job losses without impeding your financial success.

Typical Techniques for Budgeting

Many different budgeting techniques might assist you in efficiently managing your finances. Here are some points to consider:

    a. **Envelope System:** This method entails setting aside money in separate envelopes for every area of expenditure. You cannot make any further purchases in a certain category until the next budgetary month if the money in an envelope is depleted. Spending discretionary money can be effectively managed using this technique.

    b. **Pay Yourself First:** By seeing savings as a fixed obligation that must be covered before other expenses or discretionary spending, this technique puts savings first. You may make sure that your savings objectives are satisfied before other costs take up your money by "paying yourself first."

    c. **Expense Tracking applications:** You can keep an eye on your spending, organize your costs, and stick to your budget with the aid of a variety of budgeting applications. These applications often connect with your credit cards and bank accounts, which makes it simpler to keep an eye on your financial behavior in real time.

d. **50/30/20 Rule:** As previously said, this guideline offers a straightforward and efficient method for allocating your money between necessities, desires, and savings. It is very helpful for those who would rather budget in an uncomplicated way.

Your financial plan is built on the Budgeting Formula. You can take charge of your finances and make sure that your money is working for you by keeping an account of your earnings and outlays, classifying your spending, establishing budgetary constraints, and routinely evaluating and modifying your budget. By creating a budget, you can control your spending, keep out of debt, and remain on course to meet your financial objectives.

Chapter 6

The Debt Management Formula

"Taking control of your finances and setting out on a path to resilience and financial freedom is more important than getting rid of debt."

Depending on how it is handled, debt may be both an asset and a liability. While certain debts—such as mortgages or school loans—can be wise investments in your future, other debts, especially consumer debt with high interest rates, have the potential to swiftly spiral out of control and undermine your financial objectives.

The Debt Management Formula is intended to assist you in comprehending, controlling, and eventually getting rid of debt, freeing up funds to help you accumulate wealth and secure your financial future.

Debt Management's Significance

Sustaining financial health requires effective debt management. Debt may assist you in reaching significant life goals, like house ownership or furthering your education if managed responsibly. Mismanaged debt, however, may result in stress, high interest rates, and little room for maneuvering financially. You can lower interest rates, raise your credit score, and increase your options for saving and investing by managing your debt well.

The Debt Management Formula's Elements

The Debt Management Formula, like other formulas, is composed of four essential parts:

1. **Being Aware of Your Debt**

    Acquiring a comprehensive knowledge of your debt is the first step towards controlling it. Making a list of all of your debts entails determining their total amounts, interest rates, minimum payments, and periods. Here's how to comprehend all of your debts:

    - **Making a List of Your Debts:** Begin by enumerating all of your debts, including credit card balances, mortgages, auto loans, school loans, and any other personal loans. Names of creditors, current balances, interest rates, minimum monthly payments, and due dates for each loan should all be included. Your approach to managing your debt will be built upon this extensive list.

    - **Interest Rates and Terms:** It is essential to comprehend the interest rates and terms of each loan. If you don't prioritize paying off debts with high interest rates, like credit cards, you may end yourself paying a lot more in total. Variable-rate loans include additional risk if interest rates rise and your monthly payments increase.

The debt-to-income (DTI) ratio may be computed by taking the entire amount of monthly debt payments and dividing it by the gross monthly income. Your capacity to save, invest, or get new credit may be hampered by a high debt-to-income ratio, which shows that a significant amount of your income is being used for debt repayment. Generally speaking, a good DTI ratio is under 36%.

2. **Giving Payback of Debt Priority**
Setting priorities for which bills to pay off first comes when you have a clear view of your debt. There are several approaches to making debt repayment a priority, and each has benefits of its own.
- **The Avalanche strategy:** Under this strategy, you pay off your debts in order of priority, paying the smallest amount owed on the loans with the highest interest rates first. After repaying the loan

with the highest interest rate, you go to the next highest. Long-term savings may be achieved by using this strategy, which reduces the overall amount of interest paid.

- **The Snowball Method:** Using this technique, you pay off the debt with the lowest amount first, regardless of interest rate, and then make the required minimum payments on the other debts. You settle the lowest loan first, then the next smallest. By offering you rapid rewards, this approach gives you psychological drive and may help you keep up the pace as you take on more significant obligations.

- **Hybrid Approach:** The avalanche and snowball approaches are combined in a hybrid approach. To get both financial and psychological rewards, you may, for instance, concentrate on paying off a modest, high-interest loan first. This method is adaptable and may be adjusted to fit your particular needs.
Consolidating debt into a single loan with a reduced interest rate might be

advantageous for those who have several high-interest loans. Consolidating your debt might simplify payments and lower your total interest expenses, but it's crucial to avoid taking on additional debt after consolidation.

3. **Applying Techniques for Debt Reduction**
Now that you've prioritized your debts, it's important to put methods in place to lower and eventually pay them off. This includes paying more than what is required, settling disputes with creditors, and maybe restructuring your debt.

- **Making Extra Payments:** Pay off your highest-priority debt as much as you can, whenever you can. The amount of interest paid overall and the time it takes to pay off a loan may both be considerably lowered with even modest extra payments. To make higher payments, think about using windfalls like bonuses, tax returns, or side income.

- **Reaching out to Creditors:** If you're having trouble paying your bills, try negotiating better terms with your creditors. Creditors can agree to a reduction in your interest rate, your monthly payment, or a lump-sum payment that is less than the whole amount owed. Successful negotiations may help you avoid default and manage your debt more effectively.

Debt restructuring is an option to consider if you are unable to make your debt payments on time. To make payments more manageable, this entails changing the conditions of your loan, such as extending the payback time or lowering the interest rate. Restructuring your debt might result in longer repayment times and higher interest rates overall, so proceed with caution.

- **Debt Management Plans:** Assisting in the creation of a debt management plan (DMP) may require consulting a credit counseling organization. Your debts are combined into a single monthly payment with a DMP, and that amount is then divided among your creditors. To help you pay off your debt more quickly, credit counselors may often negotiate reduced interest rates and fees on your behalf.

4. **Steer clear of debt in the future**
   It's not enough to only manage and get rid of your present debt. Steer clear of debt if you want to attain long-term financial stability. To do this, cultivate the following routines and tactics to encourage budgetary restraint and ward against overspending:

   - **Establishing an Emergency Fund:** Unexpected costs, such as auto or medical bills, are a major contributing factor to debt for many individuals. You may pay for these expenditures without using credit cards or loans if you accumulate an emergency fund equal to three to six months' worth of living expenses.

   - **Living Within Your Means:** Make sure that, by following your budget, your expenses and income are in line. Instead of spending more money as your salary improves, avoid lifestyle inflation and use any additional cash for debt reduction, investments, or savings.

   - **Making Responsible Use of Credit:** If you use credit cards, make sure you pay the whole amount off each month. Steer clear of carrying a balance since the interest may mount up rapidly. If you tend to overspend, you may want to use debit cards or cash for regular expenditures.

- **Avert Unnecessary Debt:** Exercise caution while taking out additional loans, particularly for luxuries. Consider if you need the item before financing it and whether you can afford it without taking out a loan. If taking on debt is necessary, compare interest rates and conditions before making a purchase.

- **Credit Monitoring:** Verify that there are no inaccuracies or fake accounts by routinely reviewing your credit report. Keeping an eye on your credit score may also help you understand how your financial choices influence it and how that may affect your future borrowing capacity.

In conclusion, the Debt Management Formula is an effective instrument for regaining control over your financial situation. You may liberate yourself from the weight of debt and lay a strong basis for financial stability by being aware of your obligations, making repayment of your debt a priority, putting effective debt reduction techniques into practice, and staying away from more debt.

Chapter 7

The Insurance Formula

"Insurance is the quiet guardian of your future, providing a cushion of certainty in a world of unpredictability."

The foundation of financial stability is insurance. It serves as a safety net to shield you, your loved ones, and your possessions against unforeseen circumstances that may otherwise wipe out your bank account.

The Significance of Insurance
Unexpected occurrences like diseases, accidents, natural catastrophes, or even death may have a big financial impact since life is unpredictable. By transferring risk from you to an insurance provider, insurance helps to prevent you from bearing the whole financial burden of these occurrences. Having the right insurance may save you a little setback from turning into a financial disaster, enabling you to bounce back and keep your stability.

The Insurance Formula's Elements
There are four main parts to the Insurance Formula:
1. **Recognizing the Dangers**
   Determine which hazards have the potential to jeopardize your financial stability as the first

stage in the Insurance Formula. Depending on your lifestyle, stage of life, and unique circumstances, these risks may change.

- **Personal Risks:** These include hazards associated with your well-being, earnings, and lifespan. What would happen, for instance, if you became sick or hurt and couldn't work? If you died suddenly, how would your family manage financially? A further personal danger is the possibility of having to pay for long-term care as one ages.

- **Property Risks:** These refer to dangers to your tangible assets, like your house, vehicle, or other priceless belongings. Significant damage or loss may result from theft, accidents, and natural catastrophes, necessitating costly repairs or replacements.

- **Liability hazards:** The potential for being held accountable for causing damage to other people or their property gives rise to liability hazards. For instance, you can be responsible for damages, attorney fees, and medical costs if someone is hurt on your property or if you get into an automobile accident.

- **Company Risks:** Owning a company exposes you to extra risks including litigation, property damage, and injury to employees. Insurance for your business may assist reduce these risks and safeguard your livelihood.

2. **Selecting the Appropriate Insurance Types**
Selecting the insurance policies that would provide the required protection is the next step after determining the dangers you encounter. There are several insurance kinds to take into account, each with a distinct function.

- **Health Insurance:** Prescription drugs, hospital stays, doctor visits, and surgery are all covered by health insurance. It's critical for guaranteeing access to required therapies and safeguarding against the exorbitant expenditures of healthcare. Screenings and vaccines are examples of preventative treatments that may sometimes be covered by health insurance.

- **Life Insurance:** In the case of your death, life insurance pays out a sum of money to your beneficiaries. If you have dependents on your salary, it's very crucial. Life insurance may assist with debt repayment, burial expenses, and financial assistance for your loved ones. Term life insurance, which gives coverage for a predetermined time, and whole life insurance, which offers lifetime coverage and may contain a savings component, are the two primary forms of life insurance.

- **Disability Insurance:** If a sickness or accident prevents you from working, disability insurance covers a part of your income. Long-term disability insurance offers coverage for longer periods than short-term disability insurance, which only covers transient ailments. If you become unemployed, having this kind of insurance is essential to preserving your financial security.

- **Renters' or homeowners' insurance:** Homeowners' insurance protects your home's contents and structure from perils, including fire, theft, and natural catastrophes. Liability insurance is also included in case someone is hurt on your property. Renters insurance offers liability protection and comparable coverage for those who rent their houses. It also protects personal goods.

- **Auto Insurance:** This kind of insurance pays for the costs incurred in auto accidents, such as damage to your automobile, medical bills, and responsibility for other people's injuries or property damage. Auto insurance is necessary for safeguarding your finances while driving and is mandated by law in many states.

- **Liability Insurance:** If you are sued for causing harm or property damage, your personal liability insurance will pay for your defense costs and damages. An extra layer of liability protection known as umbrella insurance comes into play when the limitations of your previous policies are reached.

- **Company Insurance:** If you are a company owner, you may need a variety of insurance policies, including liability, workers' compensation, and property insurance. If a covered occurrence prevents your firm from operating for a brief period, business interruption insurance may also shield you against lost revenue.

- **Long-Term Care Insurance:** This kind of insurance pays for care expenses such as nursing home care, home healthcare, and help with daily tasks that are often not covered by health insurance. This kind of insurance is especially crucial as you become older and need assistance with daily tasks.

3. **Establishing Sufficient Coverage**

   It's not enough to just get the correct kind of insurance; you also need to be sure that your coverage levels are high enough to shield you from future losses. However, the following must be taken into account to calculate the appropriate coverage:

- **Determining the Worth of Your Assets:** Find out how much your house, vehicle, and other valuables would cost to replace to get property insurance. Verify that, in the case of a complete loss, your coverage will allow you to restore or replace these assets.

- **Calculating Income Needs:** When purchasing life and disability insurance, take into account how much your family would need to make ends meet if you were unable to do so. Take into account your debts, upcoming costs (such as college tuition), and the current living expenditures of your family.

- **Assessing Liability Risks:** When evaluating liability insurance, take into account the probable expenditures of a lawsuit, such as settlement costs, court costs, and lost wages. If you own substantial assets, you may want to think about getting umbrella insurance to extend your liability coverage over the limitations of your regular policy.

- **Taking Health and Long-Term Care Needs Into Account:** Based on your age, family history, and health history, assess your possible medical and care needs for health and long-term care insurance. Select a plan that will safeguard you from large out-of-pocket costs and yet provide you access to the treatment you need.

4. **Consistently Examining and Changing Your Policies**

   As your circumstances vary over time, so will your insurance requirements. To make sure your insurance plans still suit your requirements, it's critical to check and update them regularly.

   - **Life Events:** The requirement for insurance may be greatly impacted by major life events like marriage, having a kid, purchasing a house, or launching a company. Check your insurance to make sure your coverage is still sufficient after any major changes.

   - **Policy Adjustments:** You may need to modify your coverage limits when you gain additional assets, settle debt, or have a change in income. For instance, you could want less life insurance if your mortgage is paid off, or you might wish to raise your disability insurance coverage if your salary rises.

- **Market changes:** A review of your policies may also be necessary in response to changes in the insurance market, including the introduction of new products, modifications to prices, or weakening of your insurer's finances. Make sure you're receiving the best deal by occasionally comparing prices and coverage choices by shopping around.

- **Health Changes:** You may need to renew your health, life, or long-term care insurance as you become older or if your health changes. Verify that you are sufficiently insured and that your plans continue to meet your requirements.

To sum up, the Insurance Formula is an essential part of financial stability since it protects your assets and provides coverage against unexpected circumstances. You can make sure that you and your loved ones are financially secure no matter what life throws at you by choosing the appropriate coverage and periodically evaluating your plans. Effective insurance planning aims to provide you stability and peace of mind for the future, not only to reduce risks.

Chapter 8

The Tax Optimization Formula

"Tax optimization is an artistic endeavor that transforms the burden of taxation into an opportunity for sustained financial gain."

Your financial picture is heavily influenced by taxes, which affect your income, investments, and the total amount of wealth that you accumulate. The purpose of the Tax Optimization Formula is to reduce your tax burden while maintaining legal compliance. You may maximize your financial resources and keep a larger portion of your income by carefully managing your taxes.

The Value of Optimizing Taxes
It is vital to optimize taxes for several reasons:
- **Maximizing Income:** You may save more of your income for savings, investments, or consumption when you lower your tax obligation.
- **Improving Investment Returns:** Careful tax preparation may increase the post-tax returns on your assets, facilitating more economic wealth accumulation.

- **Achieving Financial Objectives:** Reduced taxes free up more cash for significant purchases, education, retirement savings, and other financial objectives.
- **Preventing Penalties:** Careful tax preparation guarantees adherence to tax regulations, assisting you in avoiding fines and interest for errors or omissions.

The Tax Optimization Formula's Components

The Tax Optimization Formula consists of four main parts:

1. **Recognizing Your Tax Duties**

   Knowing the various forms of income and how they are taxed is the first step toward optimizing your taxes. You may use this information to take advantage of possible tax advantages and make well-informed choices.

   - **Income Types:** Tax rates vary depending on the kind of income. For instance, the marginal income tax rate applies to ordinary income, which includes wages and salaries. Profits from the sale of assets, or capital gains, may be liable to reduced tax rates based on the length of time you've owned the asset (short-term vs. long-term). In addition, interest income, dividends, and rental income have different tax consequences.

- **Tax Brackets:** Because income tax rates are progressive, greater incomes are subject to higher rates of taxation. Knowing your tax bracket enables you to plan for taxes and take actions, such as making contributions to retirement accounts, that lower your taxable income.

- **Credits and Deductions:** Tax credits immediately lower your tax payment, while tax deductions lower your taxable income. To optimize your tax advantages, familiarize yourself with typical credits and deductions (such as education credits, energy-efficient home upgrades, and mortgage interest).

- **Taxable vs. Non-Taxable Income:** Certain gifts and inheritances, interest on municipal bonds, and payments from life insurance are examples of income sources that are not liable to income tax. You can make better plans if you know which of your revenue streams are exempt from taxes.

2. **Making Use of Tax Benefit Accounts**
   Special tax advantages are provided by tax-advantaged accounts, which may lower your taxable income and boost your worth. These accounts are intended to promote investing and saving by offering tax advantages.

   - **Retirement Accounts:** You may lower your taxable income by making contributions to retirement accounts like 403(b)s, Traditional and Roth IRAs, and 401(k)s. While Roth retirement accounts require post-tax contributions but allow for tax-free withdrawals in retirement, standard retirement account contributions are made using pre-tax cash, reducing your current taxable income.

   - **Health Savings Accounts (HSAs):** HSAs provide you with tax benefits while allowing you to save money for medical costs. Tax deductions are available for contributions, and withdrawals used for approved medical costs are free of taxes. Any investment gains made in the HSA also increase tax-free.

- **Flexible Spending Accounts (FSAs):** With an FSA, you may reserve pre-tax money for qualified medical and dependent care costs. Your taxable income is decreased by contributions, and withdrawals made for approved expenditures are tax-free.

- **Education Savings Accounts:** Tax advantages are offered for educational costs via accounts such as Coverdell Education Savings Accounts and 529 schemes. Certain states allow for the deduction of 529 plan contributions, and profits grow tax-free when applied to eligible educational costs.

- **Investment Accounts:** Under some circumstances, tax-advantaged investment accounts, like some forms of life insurance or annuities, provide advantages like tax-deferred growth or tax-free withdrawals.

3. **Putting Tax-Efficient Plans Into Practice**
You may reduce taxes on your investments and other income streams by using tax-efficient practices. These tactics are designed to maximize

your investment returns while lowering your total tax obligation.

- **Tax-Loss Harvesting:** In this tactic, assets are sold at a loss to balance profits from other investments. You may be able to minimize your taxable capital gains and your tax obligation by incurring losses.

- **Asset Location:** Invest in accounts that correspond to the tax treatment of your holdings. Put assets with greater tax loads, like bonds, in tax-advantaged accounts and tax-efficient investments, such as index funds or municipal bonds, in taxable accounts.

- **Qualified Dividends vs. Non-Qualified Dividends:** The tax rate on qualified dividends is lower than that of non-qualified dividends. Purchase qualifying dividend-paying equities to take advantage of these reduced rates.
- Income Splitting: To benefit from lower tax bands, income is divided among family members via income splitting. One way to lessen the total family tax

obligation is to donate assets to children or other family members who are in lower tax categories.

- **Charitable Giving:** Giving valuable assets to a good cause might have two advantages. In addition to receiving a charitable deduction for the fair market value of the given assets, you may avoid paying capital gains taxes on the appreciation.

4. **Organization and Documentation**
Meticulous preparation and precise documentation are essential for successful tax optimization. Making well-informed choices throughout the year is facilitated by proper preparation, and maintaining accurate records guarantees that your tax credits and deductions can be supported.

- **Tax Planning:** Create a tax plan at the start of the year or whenever there are major alterations to your finances. Take into account variables, including anticipated income, credits, and deductions, when making choices that will lower your tax obligation.

- **Monitoring Income and Expenses:** Maintain thorough records of your earnings, outlays, and financial commitments. Keep records of all credits, deductions, and other tax-related matters. Your tax return preparation and any claims you make in the case of an audit will be made simpler as a result.

- **Using Tax Software or Specialist Assistance:** To make preparing your tax return easier, think about using tax software. For more complicated cases, get advice from a tax specialist. Tax experts may provide you with individualized guidance and assist you in successfully navigating the tax code.

- **Examining Tax Returns:** Make sure your tax returns are accurate and comprehensive regularly. To minimize your tax advantages and prevent penalties, be sure that all income, credits, and deductions are recorded accurately.

Financial security is significantly influenced by strategic tax planning. This is because it makes the most of your income and investment returns while also facilitating the more effective attainment of your financial objectives. As a result, the Tax Optimization Formula is an essential part of efficient money management.

Chapter 9

The Retirement Planning Formula

"Retirement is the beginning of a new chapter, written with the wisdom of your past and the freedom you've earned through careful planning," rather than the conclusion of your journey."

Retirement Planning: What Is It?

The process of preparing for your financial stability and lifestyle requirements in the years when you are not employed is known as retirement planning. It entails deciding on a retirement lifestyle and taking action to guarantee you have the finances to maintain it.

As such, it is essential to safeguard your financial future and guarantee a decent retirement.

What is the purpose of the Retirement Planning Formula?

To attain a financially secure retirement, retirement planning entails evaluating your requirements, establishing objectives, and putting plans into action. It is methodically created to help people get ready for retirement and make sure they have the money to maintain their ideal level of life.

The Value of Making Retirement Plans

Planning for retirement effectively is essential for many reasons:

a. **Financial Security:** Making the right plans will guarantee that you have enough money to meet your needs and sustain your lifestyle in retirement.

b. **Peace of Mind:** Having a well-thought-out strategy eases your mind about the future and allows you to enjoy retirement stress-free.

c. **Goal Achievement:** Whether it's traveling, engaging in hobbies, or providing for family members, retirement planning aids in the setting and realization of financial objectives.

d. **Protection Against Inflation:** An all-inclusive retirement plan takes inflation into account, guaranteeing that your buying power will be steady over time.

The Elements of the Formula for Retirement Planning

The four main parts of the retirement planning formula are as follows:

1. **Evaluating Needs for Retirement**

Planning starts with figuring out how much money you'll need in retirement. This entails projecting your future spending and considering inflation and healthcare costs. The following elements influence how much money you will need for a comfortable retirement.

- **Projecting Future Expenses:** Take into account the costs you expect to incur after you retire, such as housing, utilities, food, transportation, medical care, entertainment, and travel. Determine whether these costs will go up or down in comparison to what you were paying before retirement.

- **Inflation:** Over time, inflation reduces the buying power of money. To guarantee that your retirement funds will keep up with growing expenses, account for an average rate of inflation.

- **Healthcare Costs:** The amount you set aside for healthcare may have a big influence on your retirement savings. Compute your prospective insurance premiums, out-of-pocket spending, and long-term care costs. Take into account the possibility that these costs may increase as you become older.

- **Longevity:** Take your life expectancy into account while making retirement plans. Assuming a longer retirement time is a wise move to prevent outliving your funds.

2. **Creating Retirement Objectives**

Establishing specific retirement objectives helps in figuring out how much you must invest and save. Your objectives have to coincide with the time and lifestyle you envision for retirement. The methods listed below might help you specify your retirement goals and objectives, including your ideal retirement age and lifestyle expectations.

- **Desired Retirement Age:** Establish your intended retirement date. The length of time you have to save and the duration of your savings will depend on when you want to retire.

- **Expectations for Your Lifestyle:** Think about the kind of life you want to lead after you retire. Travel, pastimes, and other activities fall within this category. Decide whether you wish to have an extravagant, modest, or balanced lifestyle.

- **Retirement Income Sources:** Determine your options for retirement income, including investments, Social Security, pensions, and retirement accounts. Calculate the expected income from each of these sources and how they will fit into your overall retirement strategy.

- **Financial Milestones:** Establish clear benchmarks for yourself to monitor your progress, including hitting a savings goal or a set return on investment.

3. **Putting Investment and Savings Plans Into Practice**

It takes both wise investment and diligent saving to accumulate sizeable retirement savings. When creating a plan to gradually increase and build your retirement funds, the following should be taken into account:

- **Retirement Accounts:** Fund retirement accounts, including Roth, IRA, and 401(k) accounts. Profit from the tax advantages and employer-matching contributions linked to these accounts.

- **Investment Strategy:** Align your retirement funds with your time horizon and risk tolerance by building a diverse portfolio. To balance growth and risk, take into account a variety of stocks, bonds, mutual funds, and other assets.

- **Regular Contributions:** As your income increases, raise the amount you save from your retirement accounts regularly. Contributions should be automated to guarantee steady savings.

- **Adapting for Risk:** Modify your investing plan progressively as you get closer to retirement to lower risk. To protect capital and provide consistent revenue, think about reallocating assets.

- **Optimizing Contributions:** If you are fifty years of age or older, make use of catch-up contributions. As you get closer to retirement, these extra contributions might help you increase your retirement savings.

4. **Making Income and Drawdown Plans**
   To make sure your funds continue during retirement, you must plan how to manage and take your income. The following should be taken into account while creating a plan for managing your income and withdrawing money:

   - **Withdrawal Strategy:** To make sure your funds survive, figure out a reasonable withdrawal rate. The standard recommendation is around 4%, although your specific situation may dictate a different amount.

   - **Social Security and Pensions:** Choose the start date for your pension and Social Security benefits. Think about how taking early or later withdrawals may affect your total retirement income.

   - **Tax Efficiency:** Take care of withdrawals from accounts that provide tax advantages in a way that minimizes taxes. To reduce your tax obligation, consider how to withdraw funds from taxable, tax-deferred, and tax-free accounts.

- **Managing Longevity Risk:** If you're looking for a lifelong income guarantee, take into account products like annuities. This might lessen the possibility that you will outlive your money.

- **Estate Planning:** Combine your estate and retirement plans. Make sure your beneficiaries are correctly identified and that your assets are dispersed according to your preferences.

To achieve a safe and enjoyable retirement, following the retirement planning formula is often necessary. Furthermore, careful preparation and methodical execution will guarantee that you have the money to live the retirement you've always wanted.

Chapter 10

The Formula for Building Wealth

"Being wealthy involves more than just accumulating wealth; it also involves developing self-control, having a clear goal, and persistently pursuing expansion. Real wealth is created one deliberate choice at a time."

Building wealth is a long-term process that entails increasing and developing your financial holdings to become financially secure and independent. The Wealth Building Formula offers a methodical strategy for gradually building wealth with an emphasis on working, saving, investing, and prudent money management.

The Value of Creating Wealth
Building wealth is important for several reasons:
I. **Financial Independence:** Developing wealth enables you to become financially independent, giving you the flexibility to make decisions unhindered by financial constraints.

II. **Security and Stability:** Building money gives you a safety net that helps you deal with unforeseen costs, downturns in the economy, and other financial difficulties.

III. **Goal Achievement:** You may accomplish both short- and long-term financial objectives, including house ownership, college financing, or a comfortable retirement, with the aid of a sound wealth-building strategy.

IV. **Generational Wealth:** Creating wealth helps support your family's financial stability and leave a legacy by securing money for the next generations.

The Elements of the Formula for Building Wealth

The Wealth Building Formula is made up of four essential parts:

1. **Raising the Potential for Earnings**

    One essential first step in accumulating money is to raise your earning capacity. A higher income speeds up the process of accumulating wealth by providing more options for savings and investments.

    The methods listed below will increase your income and improve your financial prospects.
    - **Professional Growth:** Invest in your career by going back to school, becoming certified, or learning new skills.

Promotions, better-paying jobs, and more work stability may result from this.

- **Side Projects and Freelance Work:** Investigate supplementary revenue sources using side projects or freelance labor. This may apply to occupations in the gig economy, internet enterprises, and consultancy. Side gig earnings may be invested in or utilized to increase savings.

- **Entrepreneurship:** Launching your own company has the potential to generate a sizable income. Create a business plan to pursue entrepreneurial endeavors once you have identified possibilities in your field of competence or interest.

- **Negotiation Skills:** Develop your capacity to bargain for higher compensation packages or pay raises. Prepare to make the case for increased compensation based on your performance and talents by researching industry norms.

2. **Efficient Techniques for Saving**
Saving regularly is a must for accumulating money. You may reach your financial objectives

and collect money for investments with the aid of efficient saving techniques.

The ways to steadily save and establish a solid financial base are as follows.

- **Budgeting:** To keep track of your earnings and outlays, develop and adhere to a budget. Make sure you live within your means by setting aside a percentage of your salary for investments and savings.

- **Emergency Fund:** Set aside three to six months' worth of living costs in an emergency fund. In the event of unforeseen circumstances, such as job loss or medical difficulties, this fund offers a safety net.

- **Automated Savings:** Configure recurring deposits to investment and savings accounts. You can continuously save and invest without having to think about it if you automate your savings.

- **Debt Reduction:** Pay off high-interest debts first, including credit card debt. Paying off debt increases your available funds for investing and saving, which supports your attempts to accumulate wealth.

3. **Investing Strategically**

Investing is a vital part of creating money. The process of strategic investing entails choosing assets that complement your risk appetite and financial objectives. These are some strategies for increasing your money via astute investing decisions.

- **Diversification:** Spread out your assets over many asset groups, including commodities, equities, bonds, and real estate. Diversification raises possible profits and aids with risk management.

- **Long-Term View:** Take a long-term approach to investing. Steer clear of rash judgments based on transient market swings and instead concentrate on long-term growth.

- **Retirement Accounts:** Make contributions to IRAs, Roth IRAs, and 401(k)s, among other retirement accounts. To optimize the growth of your investments, make use of employer-matching contributions and tax advantages.

- **Regular payments:** Even if you only make little payments regularly, be sure to fund your investing accounts. Compound interest, when paired with consistent investment, may result in substantial wealth creation over time.

- **Investment Education:** Keep up your knowledge of investment possibilities and tactics. Keep up with market developments and, if necessary, consult financial experts for help.

4. **Growth and Financial Management**

Maintaining your financial objectives and growing your wealth are guaranteed by practicing effective money management. The following is a list of strategies for handling your money wisely and guaranteeing that your business grows:

- **Monitoring and Modifying:** Examine your investment portfolio and financial strategy regularly. As your ambitions, the market, or your financial status change, make the necessary adjustments.

- **Tax Efficiency:** To reduce your tax bill, put tax-efficient investing ideas into practice. This involves knowing the tax ramifications of various assets and making use of tax-advantaged accounts.

- **Estate Planning:** Make arrangements via estate planning for the transfer of your fortune. Create trusts, wills, and other estate planning instruments to guarantee that your assets are allocated as per your desires and reduce inheritance taxes.

- **Financial Milestones and Goals:** Establish clear financial objectives and monitor your progress toward reaching them. Evaluate your progress toward your goals regularly and make any adjustments to your tactics.

You may attain your financial objectives and create enduring wealth by raising your earning capacity, putting sensible saving plans into place, making calculated investments, and handling your money well.

Note: Building wealth is an ongoing process that calls for preparation, knowledge, and self-control, but the benefits are well worth the work.

Chapter 11

The Financial Education Formula

"The first step in achieving financial literacy is acquiring financial literacy, which is essential for making informed choices and securing one's future."

A key component of financial stability is **Financial Literacy**. Making wise and sensible judgments about money management, however, requires knowledge of financial ideas, instruments, and tactics. It is thus essential to successful money management and long-term financial success.

What is included in the financial education formula?

A methodical strategy for gaining the information and abilities required to make wise financial choices, accumulate money, and safeguard your financial future is outlined in the Financial Education Formula.

Why is financial education crucial?

- It gives you the ability to make wise financial choices.

- It aids people in comprehending financial ideas that are necessary for risk management and avoiding mistakes.
- Gaining knowledge about finance gives you the power to expand and safeguard your possessions.
- It makes it possible for people to become and stay financially independent.

The Elements of the Formula for Financial Education

The four main parts of the Financial Education Formula are as follows:

1. **Recognizing the Fundamentals of Finance**
   To make wise selections, one must have a firm understanding of fundamental financial concepts. The following should be taken into account while learning the foundations of financial concepts:
   - **Budgeting:** To keep track of your income and spending, learn how to make and stick to a budget. Recognize the significance of budgeting and living within your means.

   - **Saving:** Recognize the fundamentals of saving, such as the significance of accumulating emergency funds and allocating funds for both immediate and long-term objectives.

- **Debt Management:** Acquire knowledge of various debt kinds, interest rates, and repayment plans. Create a strategy for efficient debt management and reduction.

- **Credit:** Recognize how credit works, including credit reports and ratings, and how credit affects financial choices. Discover how to establish and preserve excellent credit.

2. **Acquiring Knowledge of Investing Techniques**
   Gaining expertise in investments is essential for building money and making long-term plans. The following are some different approaches to learning about different investing possibilities and approaches.

   - **Types of Investments:** Acquire knowledge about stocks, bonds, real estate, and mutual funds, among other investment possibilities. Recognize the risks and rewards connected to each kind.

   - **Investment Principles:** Learn about the time value of money, asset allocation, and diversification as fundamental concepts in investing. Find out how to use these ideas while creating a portfolio.

- **Retirement Planning:** Learn about retirement accounts, including IRAs, Roth IRAs, and 401(k)s. Recognize ways to optimize benefits and contributions.

- **Risk Management:** Develop your ability to evaluate and control investment risk. Recognize techniques for keeping the risk and return in your investing portfolio in check.

3. **Gaining Knowledge about Financial Management**

   Achieving financial success and stability requires effective money management. The following are some strategies for developing money management skills that can help you handle money wisely.

   - **Savings Strategies:** Acquire knowledge about various strategies for saving, including investment vehicles, high-yield savings accounts, and automated transfers.

- **Expense Tracking:** Learn how to keep track of and evaluate your spending. Utilize applications and tools to keep an eye on expenses and pinpoint areas that need work.

- **Financial Planning:** Learn how to set up a thorough financial plan that includes investing, saving, budgeting, and making plans for significant life events.

- **Goal Setting:** Acquire the skills necessary to establish and meet financial objectives, such as purchasing a house, paying for school, or making retirement plans.

4. **Keeping Up to Date and Adjusting**
   Being up-to-date on trends and flexible in response to changes is necessary for the continuous process of financial education. The methods listed below can help you stay current on financial trends and constantly learn new things.

   - **Lifelong Learning:** Continue your education in finance by attending conferences, webinars, books, and courses. Keep abreast of changes to laws, rules, and industry developments.

- **Adjusting to Changes:** Be ready to modify your financial strategy in response to events in your life, changes in the economy, or adjustments to your financial circumstances. Continue to be flexible and open to new information.

- **Seeking Professional Advice:** When in doubt, seek the advice of financial experts like accountants, advisors, or financial planners. They may provide professional advice and assist you in coming to wise conclusions.

To sum up, the Financial Education Formula offers a thorough method for gaining the information and abilities required for sound financial management. You may make wise judgments, accumulate wealth, and become financially independent by studying the fundamentals of finance, mastering investing techniques, honing your money management abilities, and being informed.

Remember, financial education is a lifelong process that calls for dedication and never-ending learning, but it is crucial for long-term financial stability.

Chapter 12

The Asset Protection Formula

"The capacity to protect the possessions you have worked so hard to acquire is a true sign of riches."

Protecting your financial assets from obligations, hazards, and dangers requires asset protection. The Asset Protection Formula offers a calculated method for protecting your capital against unanticipated difficulties and guaranteeing its maintenance. To successfully secure your assets, this formula places a strong emphasis on preventative actions and legal procedures.

Why Is Protecting Your Assets Important?
a. It assists in shielding your assets from creditors, future lawsuits, and other monetary dangers.
b. It guarantees your wealth's stability and security even in unfavorable circumstances.
c. It gives you comfort in knowing that your valuables are protected from dangers and possible losses.
d. It safeguards your possessions to guarantee their preservation for the next generations, and your estate is administered by your desires.

The Elements of the Formula for Asset Protection

Four essential elements make up the Asset Protection Formula.

1. **Legal Frameworks and Organizations**

    Your assets might be significantly protected by legal companies and structures. The following are some different approaches to utilizing legal entities to protect your assets from liabilities:

    - **Limited Liability Companies (LLCs):** By keeping personal and corporate funds separate, LLC formation reduces personal risk and helps protect personal assets from business obligations.

    - **Trusts:** You may protect your assets from creditors and make sure they are dispersed by your preferences by creating trusts, such as revocable or irrevocable trusts. Trusts may assist sidestep the probate procedure and provide privacy as well.

    - **Companies:** Since companies are separate legal organizations that shield their stockholders from responsibility, forming one affords security for personal assets against company defaults and liabilities.

- **Partnerships:** Properly drafted agreements and careful arrangement may help clarify responsibilities and safeguard each partner's unique assets.

2. **Protection From Insurers**

Because insurance offers financial protection against a range of dangers, it is essential for asset protection. Here are some strategies for putting suitable insurance policies into place to guard against hazards.

- **Liability Insurance:** To guard against accusations of carelessness or injury, get liability insurance. This covers insurance for product liability, professional liability, and general liability.

- **Renters' and homeowners' insurance:** Make sure your rental or house has enough coverage against liability, theft, and property damage.

- **Auto Insurance:** Keep up-to-date comprehensive auto insurance to protect against losses, injuries, and legal obligations associated with owning a car.

- **Umbrella Insurance:** If your regular policy limits aren't enough to protect you against responsibility, think about getting umbrella insurance. This insurance offers protection against a range of lawsuits and claims.

- **Health and Life Insurance:** Get life insurance to protect your dependents and pay inheritance taxes, as well as health insurance to cover medical costs.

3. **Will Arrangements**

Estate planning includes techniques to safeguard your possessions and control how they are distributed. The following are some ideas for using estate planning to successfully transfer and safeguard assets.

- **Wills:** Draft a will specifying how you want your belongings to be allocated in the event of your passing. A well-written will lessen disagreements among heirs and assist in guaranteeing that your desires are carried out.

- **Trusts:** Manage and safeguard assets both during your life and after your passing with the help of trusts. Trusts may shield assets from creditors and provide tax advantages.

- **Powers of Attorney:** Assign authority to make choices about finances and medical care. This guarantees that in the event of your incapacitation, choices may be made on your behalf by someone you trust.

- **Beneficiary Designations:** Make sure your estate plan is in line with beneficiary designations on life insurance, retirement plans, and bank accounts by updating them.

4. **Methods of Finance**

Financial techniques may guard your money and reduce risk. The following are tactics or approaches to reduce risk and safeguard your assets.

- **Asset Diversification:** To lower risk, distribute your assets across several different asset types. Diversification shields your portfolio against hazards unique to your industry and fluctuations in the market.

- **Debt Management:** To lower financial risk and manage and decrease debt. Steer clear of high-interest loans and keep your debt-to-income ratio in check.

- **Emergency Fund:** Establish a fund for unforeseen costs and difficult financial times. This fund acts as a safety net for your savings and investments.

- **Legal safeguards:** To secure assets in a variety of circumstances, make use of legal safeguards including prenuptial agreements and liability waivers.

The objective of effective asset protection is to guarantee long-term financial security and peace of mind, in addition to safeguarding your wealth from unforeseen risks. By strategically planning and diversifying your assets, you can protect your financial future, enabling you to preserve and develop your wealth for future generations.

Chapter 13

The Financial Discipline Formula

"Do you know that you may go from where you are to where you want to be in life by exercising financial discipline?"

What does it mean to be financially disciplined?

The discipline of handling your money with restraint, predictability, and control is known as financial discipline. To reach long-term financial objectives, deliberate and well-informed choices regarding investing, saving, and spending are required.

To achieve financial independence, accumulate money, and preserve financial stability, one must cultivate financial discipline.

Why Is Financial Self-Control Important?

1. **Reaching Financial Objectives:** Whether your financial objectives are long-term, like retirement, or short-term, like purchasing a vehicle, financial discipline can help you remain focused on them.

2. **Preventing Debt:** Having sound financial habits lowers your risk of taking on pointless debt and makes it easier for you to pay off what you already have.

3. **Creating Wealth:** Financial stability and wealth creation are the results of disciplined saving and investing over time.

4. **Stress Reduction:** Having a disciplined approach to money management and being ready for unforeseen costs are two ways that financial discipline helps people feel less stressed about their finances.

How to Acquire Financial Self-Control
1. Establish and Follow a Budget
- **Track Your Spending:** To determine where your money is going, start by keeping track of your earnings and outlays. Utilize applications or tools for budgeting to make this process easier.

- **Set Prudent Boundaries:** Set spending limits for many areas, including food, entertainment, and travel.

- **Review Frequently:** Make sure your budget is in line with your financial objectives and evolving situation by reviewing and adjusting it regularly.

2. Program Investments and Savings
- **Automatic Transfers:** Configure your checking account to automatically move funds to your investment and savings accounts. Setting up an automated savings account helps you stay consistent and achieve your financial objectives.

- **Retirement Contributions:** Fund retirement accounts regularly, including IRAs or 401(k)s. You may benefit from tax advantages and compound growth by automating these donations.

3. Clearly Define Your Financial Objectives
- **Establish Your Objectives:** Decide on SMART (specific, measurable, attainable, relevant, and time-bound) financial objectives. This might be setting up an emergency fund, paying off debt, or saving for a trip.

- **Make a Strategy:** Create a thorough strategy with deadlines and milestones to help you reach your objectives. Divide more ambitious objectives into more doable, smaller stages.

4. **Establish Resilient Spending Practices**
    - **Prevent Impulse Purchases:** Put techniques in place to prevent impulsive purchases, such as developing a shopping list and following it or giving yourself a full day before making non-essential purchases.

    - **Compare costs:** To make sure you are receiving the most value for your money, shop about and compare costs before making big purchases.

    - **Use Cash:** To better manage your finances and prevent overpaying on credit cards, think about making discretionary purchases using cash.

5. **Control and Lower Debt**
    - **Make Debt Repayment a Priority:** Pay off credit card debt and other high-interest debts first. To decrease debt methodically, think about using techniques like the debt avalanche or snowball.

    - **Avoid additional Debt:** Unless essential, refrain from taking on additional debt. Use credit wisely and stick to your budget while making purchases.

6. **Establish and Preserve Emergency Cash**

- **Save Often:** Make recurring contributions to an emergency fund to help pay for unforeseen costs like auto or medical repairs. Set aside enough cash to pay for living costs for three to six months.

- **Keep It Accessible:** To make sure you can get to your emergency money immediately in an emergency, keep it in a liquid, readily accessible account, such as a savings account.

7. Get Knowledgeable About Personal Finances
- **Read Books and Articles:** To expand your financial literacy and keep up with industry trends and tactics, read books and articles about personal finance.

- **Take Courses:** To learn about investing, budgeting, and other financial matters, sign up for seminars or courses in financial education.

- **Consult specialists:** To get information and direction unique to your financial circumstances, consult specialists such as financial advisers.

8. Track Your Economic Development
- **Regular Reviews:** To monitor your progress and make any required modifications, evaluate your

financial strategy, budget, and investment performance regularly.

- **Celebrate Milestones:** To maintain motivation and promote sound financial practices, recognize and celebrate reaching financial milestones.

Getting Past Financial Temptation

Your ambitions might be derailed and your financial discipline compromised by financial temptation. It often entails the impulse to spend money carelessly or to make financial mistakes that are counterproductive to your long-term goals. It takes self-awareness and tactics to resist financial temptation so that you may make more thoughtful and prudent financial decisions.

Recognizing Financial Temptation

a. **Triggers:** Recognize the factors, such as stress, peer pressure, or marketing strategies, that might lead to financial temptation.

b. **Emotional Spending:** Understand how feelings of enthusiasm, boredom, or aggravation may lead to impulsive purchases.

c. **Marketing Influence:** Recognize how promotions and ads may instill a feeling of urgency in you and affect your choices to buy.

Techniques for Resisting Financial Temptation

1. **Establish and adhere to a budget**
   - **Set Limits:** Decide how much money may be spent on certain things, including shopping, entertainment, and eating out. A well-defined budget keeps your money in check and helps you avoid overpaying.

   - **Track Expenses:** Keep a close eye on your spending to make sure you are adhering to your spending plan. Use applications or tools for budgeting to keep track of and control your expenditures.

2. **Establish a Budget**
   - **Give Needs More Weight Than Desired:** Make a distinction between necessities and desires. Prioritize meeting your necessities, then, within the limits of your budget, set aside money for your desires.

   - **Plan Acquisitions:** Create a list of the things you want to buy and follow it.

Steer clear of impulsive purchases that go against your goal.

3. **Give the 24-hour Rule effect.**
    - **Pause Before Purchasing:** Give yourself a full day to consider a purchase before acting on an impulse. This gives you time to consider if the purchase is really necessary and lessens the chance that you will regret it.

    - **Assess Impact:** Take into account how the purchase will affect your long-term financial objectives and if it fits within your priorities and budget.

4. **Use Debit Cards or Cash**
    - **Steer Clear of Credit Cards:** To lower the chance of accruing debt, use credit cards sparingly for impulsive purchases. For regular transactions, use debit cards or cash to have greater control over your spending.

    - **Establish Spending limitations:** To avoid overspending while using credit cards, establish spending limitations and keep an eye on your transactions.

5. **Issue a Challenge for Savings**
    - **Set Savings Objectives:** Assign oneself the task of saving a certain sum of money in a predetermined period. This may support the development of sound financial habits and help you change your attention from spending to saving.

    - **Track Progress:** To remain inspired and dedicated to your financial goals, keep track of your progress toward your savings target and recognize accomplishments.

6. **Steer clear of enticing places**
    - **Steer Clear of Sales:** If you're prone to making impulsive purchases, steer clear of shops or websites that entice you with discounts or special offers.

    - **Unsubscribe from Emails:** To lessen your exposure to temptation, unsubscribe from marketing emails and alerts that advertise deals or new goods.

7. **Establish an Emergency Fund**

- **Set Aside Money for Unexpected Expenses:** Keeping an emergency fund on hand might help you resist the temptation to splurge on non-essential purchases. It keeps you disciplined and offers a safety net for unanticipated costs.

- **Reinforce Savings:** You may steadily increase your emergency fund without having to make deliberate choices by setting up automatic donations.

8. **Look for Support and Accountability**
    - **Share Your Goals:** Tell a trustworthy friend or relative about your financial objectives so they can support you and help you stay on track.

    - **Join a Group:** Take into consideration being a member of a community or financial responsibility group where you may talk about your objectives, obstacles, and methods for resisting temptation.

9. **Become knowledgeable**
    - **Gain Knowledge About Financial Planning:** Expand your understanding of financial management and planning.

Knowing how financial choices may affect your long-term objectives can help you stay stronger and resist temptation.

- **Remain Up to Date:** Continue your financial education by reading books and articles and attending seminars; this will help to reaffirm the value of responsible financial conduct.

Finally, acquiring financial discipline is a difficult process. To improve your financial situation, you must be consistently deliberate. However, you may achieve your financial objectives if you put all of these tactics to use.

Chapter 14

The Formula for Preserving Wealth

"Wealth preservation is about nurturing and securing a legacy that lasts through generations, anchored in wisdom and foresight, rather than just protecting what you have."

What does it mean to preserve wealth?

The deliberate practice of safeguarding and preserving an asset's worth over time is known as wealth preservation. To assure money's durability and reduce the chance of loss from a variety of sources, including market swings, inflation, taxes, and unanticipated occurrences, it entails managing and protecting wealth. Maintaining an asset's existing worth is simply one aspect of wealth preservation; another is making sure it grows and is sustainable for future generations.

It is thus crucial for preserving and safeguarding your financial assets over time.

The Value of Preserving Wealth

These are the main justifications for the significance of wealth preservation.

    I.   **Safeguarding Your Assets:** By preserving your money, you can protect it from unanticipated

catastrophes, legal challenges, and downturns in the economy.
II. **Preserving Financial Stability:** It guarantees that your money will continue to support your lifestyle and financial objectives.
III. **Safeguarding Future Generations:** It maintains your money to leave a lasting legacy and support future generations.
IV. **Reducing hazards:** It lessens the possibility of financial hazards depleting your money and upsetting your financial strategies.

The Formula for Preserving Wealth

The measures to protect your money against dangers, market volatility, and possible losses are the main emphasis of the money Preservation Formula. This method places a strong emphasis on taking preventative actions to make sure your assets are safe and continue to increase throughout your lifetime and beyond.

The Wealth Preservation Formula's Elements

The four essential elements of the Wealth Preservation Formula are as follows:
1. **Diversification**
   Investing across a variety of asset classes via diversification is a crucial wealth preservation strategy. To lower risk, you may diversify your

assets among a variety of asset types in this manner.

- **Asset Allocation:** Divide your assets across several asset types, including commodities, equities, bonds, and real estate. This lessens the effect that a single asset class's bad performance will have on your portfolio as a whole.

- **Geographic Diversification:** Spread your investments over many geographical areas to reduce the effect of regional political or economic unrest on your wealth.

- **Industry Diversification:** To guard against downturns in a particular industry and distribute investments throughout several industries or sectors.

- **Investment Vehicles:** To achieve diversity, use a variety of investment vehicles, such as individual stocks, mutual funds, and exchange-traded funds (ETFs).

2. **Managing Risks**

Managing your risks well may help shield your money from future dangers and unknowns. The following factors must be taken into account to put plans to manage and reduce financial risks into action:

- **Insurance:** To protect yourself from monetary losses resulting from unforeseen circumstances, get the right insurance coverage, such as liability, property, health, and life insurance.

- **Emergency Fund:** Keep an emergency fund liquid enough to handle unforeseen costs and financial setbacks without having to sell assets.

- **Hedging Techniques:** To guard against any losses in your investing portfolio, think about using hedging techniques like options or futures contracts.

- **Risk Assessment:** Continually evaluate and modify your risk exposure in response to changes in your financial circumstances, the state of the market, and your investing objectives.

3. **Will Arrangements**

Managing and safeguarding your assets for future generations is part of estate planning. The following must be kept in mind to using estate planning tools to safeguard and transfer your assets:

- **Wills:** Draft a will to outline the distribution of your assets in the event of your passing. A will may lessen disagreements among heirs and assist in guaranteeing that your desires are followed.

- **Trusts:** To manage and safeguard your assets, create trusts, such as irrevocable or revocable trusts. Benefits from trusts include tax savings, asset preservation, and probate avoidance.

- **Powers of Attorney:** Assign authority to make choices about finances and medical care. This guarantees that in the event of your incapacitation, choices may be made on your behalf by someone you trust.

- **Beneficiary Designations:** Make sure your estate plan is in line with beneficiary designations on accounts including bank accounts, life insurance, and retirement programs.

4. **Consistent Evaluation and Modification**
Maintaining your financial plan in line with your objectives and situation requires regular reviews and adjustments. The methods listed below may help you assess and modify your financial plan regularly to accommodate changing circumstances.
- **Financial Reviews:** Review your investment portfolio, risk management techniques, and financial strategy frequently. Make modifications in response to events in your life, shifts in the market, and modifications in your financial status.

- **Portfolio Rebalancing:** To retain the asset allocation and risk tolerance that you have established, regularly rebalance your investment portfolio.

- **Tax Planning:** To reduce tax liabilities and maximize after-tax returns, put tax-efficient techniques into practice. This involves knowing the tax ramifications of various assets and making use of tax-advantaged accounts.

- **Update Estate Plans:** To take into consideration any changes in family dynamics, financial circumstances, or legal requirements, review and update your estate plan regularly.

In summary, the secret to wealth preservation is not so much what you have now as it is how you properly manage and safeguard those assets to make sure they endure and grow for the benefit of future generations.

Chapter 15

The Financial Freedom Formula

"Achieving financial independence is akin to navigating through unexplored waters; with cautious guidance and steady hands, you arrive at a shore of infinite possibilities."

What does it mean to be financially free?

Financial freedom is the ability to live life on your terms, free from financial restraints, and to confidently follow your passions and purposes in life. In other words, it serves as a doorway to a life in which your goals, not your constraints, dictate the decisions you make.

Financial freedom is significant because;
- It gives you the freedom to make decisions based on their preferences rather than their financial situation.
- It is always a financial concern, which enhances mental and emotional health.
- It offers unrestricted financial flexibility to follow one's interests, change careers, and take advantage of educational possibilities.
- It guarantees that you have enough money set aside to deal with unforeseen costs and emergencies without endangering your capacity to make ends meet.

- Finally, it allows you to leave a legacy, transfer money to the next generation, and support organizations that are important to you.

The Formula for Financial Freedom

The Financial Freedom Formula provides a methodical strategy for reaching financial freedom so you may follow your interests and have an independent life. This formula includes wealth-building, long-term sustainability planning, and money management techniques.

The Elements of the Formula for Financial Freedom

Four essential elements make up the Financial Freedom Formula:

1. **Financial planning**
   To reach your financial objectives and safeguard your financial future, this method entails managing your money via thorough analysis, strategy formulation, and continual revisions. It entails putting up a thorough plan to reach financial independence, which includes saving and investing as well as defining meaningful objectives, making a budget, and keeping track of financial plan progress.

2. **Building Wealth**

This is the process of gradually building up your financial assets by wise resource management, intelligent investment, and saving decisions. It entails coming up with and carrying out strategies to increase wealth, improve financial stability, and accomplish long-term financial objectives.

3. **Diversification of Income**

   To lower financial risk, this entails distributing your income among a variety of occupations, assets, and entrepreneurial endeavors. By spreading your income, you reduce the effect of a decline in any one source, guaranteeing a more steady and consistent flow of revenue overall. This strategy improves financial stability and guards against income loss.

4. **Eco-Friendly Lifestyle**

   Long-term financial freedom requires prudent cost and lifestyle management:

   - **Live Within Your Means:** To protect your money, spend no more than you make and steer clear of lifestyle inflation.

   - **Retirement Planning:** Establish a retirement plan that ensures sufficient resources by taking future living expenditures and healthcare demands into consideration.

- **Track Spending:** To save expenses and make the most of your financial resources, evaluate and tweak your budget regularly.

To sum up, attaining financial freedom demands dedication, self-control, and continuous oversight; yet, the benefits of being financially independent and having the capacity to follow your interests make the process valuable.

Chapter 16

The Legacy Planning Formula

"Our legacy isn't how much money we leave behind; rather, it's how we leave our mark on people's thoughts and emotions, influencing generations after us."

Legacy Planning Formula offers a thorough method for handling and safeguarding your possessions, making a significant contribution, and guaranteeing that your last desires are carried out.

It entails putting up a thorough plan to distribute and manage your assets in a manner that both upholds your moral principles and makes sure future generations benefit from your riches. To leave a lasting legacy that is in line with your life's purpose involves creating wills, trusts, and other legal structures, avoiding taxes, naming beneficiaries, and making charitable donations.

The four main parts of the Legacy Planning Formula are as follows:
1. **Estate planning**
   Organizing and managing your assets to make sure they are transferred by your desires is known as estate planning. The methods listed below

might help you create a strategy for the division of your assets.

- **Write a will:** To determine how your possessions should be distributed among your heirs, draft a will. A will clarifies your intentions and helps to prevent disagreements.

- **Create trusts:** To manage and safeguard your assets, create trusts, such as irrevocable or revocable trusts. Probate avoidance, wealth protection, and asset distribution management are just a few advantages that trusts may provide.

- **Name the recipients:** Make sure your beneficiary designations on accounts, such as bank accounts, retirement accounts, and life insurance policies, are up to date and compliant with your entire estate plan.

- **Power of attorney:** Designate someone to handle financial and medical choices if you are unable to do so for yourself. This guarantees that the people handling your affairs will follow your wishes.

2. **Efficiency in Taxation**
   By reducing the tax burden on your estate, tax efficiency measures help save a larger portion of your fortune for your heirs. These are the steps involved in putting plans in place to reduce estate taxes and other costs.
   - **Gift tax planning:** Transfer assets to beneficiaries while you are still living to lower the value of your estate by taking advantage of yearly gift tax exclusions and lifetime gift tax exemptions.

   - **Charitable contributions:** To lower estate taxes and support causes you care about, think about reducing your estate via charitable contributions made through your estate plan.

   - **Optimize asset allocation:** Arrange your assets in a way that allows you to benefit from tax-efficient investments and accounts, such as tax-free municipal bonds and tax-deferred retirement funds.

   - **Estate tax planning:** Utilize trusts and other estate planning instruments as part of a strategy to minimize estate taxes that you build with a tax professional.

3. **Charity Objectives**

   By including charitable contributions in your legacy plan, you may give back to causes and groups that have special value for you.

   - **Charitable bequests:** To allocate a part of your inheritance to charitable organizations, include charitable bequests in your will or trust.

   - **Donor-advised funds:** To make philanthropic donations over time with flexibility and perhaps to maximize tax advantages, set up a donor-advised fund.

   - **Charitable trusts:** Create charitable lead trusts or charitable remainder trusts to support charity organizations and maybe get tax benefits.

   - **Legacy of giving:** To leave a long-lasting legacy of kindness and social effect, educate and include your family in your charitable endeavors.

4. **Communication within the family**

Good communication lowers the likelihood of conflict and guarantees that your preferences are followed by your family. To guarantee that your desires are conveyed effectively;

- **Talk openly with family members about your plan:** Discuss your estate plan, including your preferences, asset distribution, and any special instructions, with your family members.

- **Plan with Heirs Involved:** Make sure your heirs are aware of your plans and ready for their obligations by including them in the planning process.

- **Update Frequently:** Periodically review and revise your estate plan to take into account changes to your financial status, personal objectives, and family dynamics.

- **Consult a Professional:** Create a thorough legacy plan that satisfies your objectives and conforms with legal standards by working with financial and legal experts.

To sum up, the Legacy Planning Formula is a methodical strategy for safeguarding and distributing your fortune in a manner consistent with your objectives and principles. Through strategic attention to estate planning, tax efficiency, charitable objectives, and family relations, you may leave a lasting legacy that helps the causes you value and benefits future generations.

CONCLUSION

Obtaining financial stability might rank among your life's most satisfying achievements. It's about developing a feeling of security, independence, and tranquility that enables you to live life on your terms, not simply about having enough money in the bank. With the information and resources found in "15 Essential Formulas to Achieve Financial Security: Tested Techniques for Generating, Preserving, and Savouring Enduring Fortune," you can take charge of your financial future.

This book's chapters each provide you with doable, practical strategies to help you establish a strong financial foundation. However, your attitude and dedication to your objectives are what matter when it comes to financial stability, not the figures and tactics. It all comes down to making sensible decisions that are compatible with your idea of a safe and happy future.

Recall that achieving financial stability is a path that calls for perseverance, self-control, and patience rather than instant success. There will be obstacles in your path, but you can overcome them if you have the correct plans and unwavering resolve. You're getting closer to the life you've imagined, one in which money is a tool to increase your pleasure and freedom rather than a cause of concern or stress, with each little step you take.

As you proceed with using the formulae in this book, remember to keep an eye on the wider picture. A life of financial stability involves not just accumulating money but also establishing a foundation of freedom to follow your passions, take care of your family, and leave a lasting legacy that is a testament to your diligence and moral character.

Apply the knowledge you have gained by taking action. Have faith in the process and your capacity to make wise financial choices. You possess the ability to construct a stable financial future that not only satisfies your needs but also gives your life meaning, happiness, and pleasure.

www.ingramcontent.com/pod-product-compliance
Lightning Source LLC
Chambersburg PA
CBHW071032240526
45469CB00006BD/2178